Medicine

Paul Dowswell

Heinemann Library
Chicago, Illinois

Customer Service 888-454-2279
Visit our website at www.heinemannlibrary.com.

Designed by Tinstar Design
Originated by Ambassador Litho
Printed by Wing King Tong in Hong Kong/China

06 05 04 03 02
10 9 8 7 6 5 4 3 2 1

Library of Congress Cataloging-in-Publication Data
Dowswell, Paul, 1957-
  Medicine / Paul Dowswell.
      p. ; cm. -- (Great inventions)
Includes bibliographical references and index.
  ISBN 1-58810-213-0 (library binding)
  1. Medicine--History--Juvenile literature. 2. Medical
innovations--History--Juvenile literature. [1. Medicine--History. 2.
Medical instruments and apparatus. 3. Medical innovations. 4.
Inventions.]
  [DNLM: 1. Equipment and Supplies--history--Juvenile Literature. 2.
Biomedical Technology--Juvenile Literature. W 26 D752m 2001] I. Title.
II. Series.
  R133.5 .D69 2001
  610'.9--dc21
                                    00-012411

Acknowledgments
The author and publishers are grateful to the following for permission to reproduce copyright material:
Cover photographs: Imagebank and Photodisc.
p. 4 Bridgeman Art Library; pp. 5, 13, 20 21 John Greim/Science Photo Library; p. 6 Michael Holford; p. 7 National Medical Slide Bank; p. 8 Corbis; pp. 9, 10, 15, 18, 25, 28, 34 Science and Society Picture Library; pp. 12, 30 A.K.G.; p. 16 Mary Evans Picture Library; p. 22 Brooks and Brown/Science Photo Library; p. 27 T.P. Orthodontics Inc.; p. 32 Marconi Ltd.; pp. 35, 37, 38 Scott Camazine/Science Photo Library; p. 39 The Wellcome Center Photolibrary; pp. 40, 41 Simon Fraser/Science Photo Library; pp. 42, 43 Science Photo Library.

Some words are shown in bold, **like this.** You can find out what they mean by looking in the glossary.

A note about dates: in this book, dates are followed by the letters B.C.E. (Before the Common Era) or C.E. (Common Era). This is instead of using the older abbreviations B.C. (Before Christ) and A.D. (*Anno Domini,* meaning "in the year of our Lord"). The date numbers are the same in both systems.

Contents

Introduction

Medicine is the art of preventing and treating disease and injury. It has a rich history of inventions. Some of these inventions, such as X-rays and stethoscopes, have made major contributions to saving lives and relieving pain. Others, such as false teeth and hearing aids, have made life more comfortable and convenient for people.

Humans have been practicing medicine since prehistoric times, but for most of history, the treatments doctors gave their patients were just as likely to kill them as to cure them. The first surgical instruments were invented to perform a radical operation called **trepanning,** where holes were drilled into the skull of a patient. This procedure was to release the evil spirits that were thought to be causing their illness.

Key inventions

Once doctors began to understand the causes of illness, they could begin to treat it much more effectively. Some of medicine's greatest discoveries have been made possible by the invention of the microscope. Light microscopes were invented in the late sixteenth century. They allowed scientists to look into a previously invisible world and discover **bacteria,** some of the most common causes of disease and infection. The invention of the electron microscope in the twentieth century led to the discovery of **viruses.** Electron microscopes also allowed researchers to unlock the secrets of our **genes.** They revealed how the tiny chemical mechanisms of **DNA** carry inherited illnesses from parent to child. The new science of **genetic engineering** promises to revolutionize medicine and provide a vast array of extraordinary cures.

*In this drawing from the early thirteenth century, a surgeon operates on a growth while the patient has to hold a basin to catch his blood. Until the nineteenth century, when **anesthetics** and antiseptics were invented, surgery was an agonizing and often fatal business.*

Seeing through you

Some inventions were put to use almost immediately. Wilhelm Roentgen's X-ray machine made headlines around the world within weeks of its development in 1895. It quickly became common in hospitals. On the other hand, the anesthetic qualities of some gases were known about for 50 years before anyone thought to use them to save patients from the pain of surgery.

Today, many of the miracles of modern medicine are so commonplace that it is easy to take them for granted. MRI and ultrasound scanners use magnetic fields and sound waves to allow doctors to see beneath our skin instantly. They detect **tumors** without the need for exploratory surgery. They can also monitor the health of a fetus in the womb with minimal inconvenience for the mother-to-be. Even when surgery is inevitable, many operations can be performed with only small incision, thanks to **fiber-optic** technology. This enables surgeons to see and manipulate tiny surgical instruments inside the body.

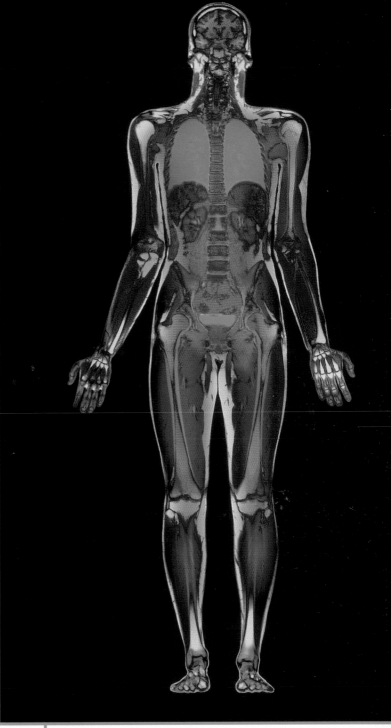

*Over the past 100 years, several inventions have made it possible for doctors to see inside the body of a patient. This extraordinary image is a whole-body MRI scan. The skeleton is clearly visible (in orange) as are **organs,** such as the lungs (in green).*

Scalpel, 3000 B.C.E.

Surgery is one of the earliest kinds of medicine known to humankind, so the scalpel is the first invention in this book. A scalpel is a small, light, and very sharp knife. It is one of the surgeon's most essential tools. It has a small, but extremely effective blade and is ideal for delicate and precise **incisions.**

Scalpels were not the first surgical instruments. These were simple stones, usually flint or obsidian, chiseled into shape by other, harder stones. The earliest ones we know of date from about 10,000 B.C.E.

Bodies in Stone Age burial sites show clear evidence of surgery. Bone setting and amputations show that early humans cared for their wounded through the healing process. Neat, round holes in the skulls of some bodies show that a radical surgical procedure called **trepanning** took place.

In this collection of medical instruments from Ancient Rome, the knife-like instrument is easy to pick out as the scalpel. This device has changed little over the centuries.

Ancient instruments

Evidence of the first-known surgical tools, including a scalpel-like bronze knife, has been found among Sumerian archaeological remains dating from around 3000 B.C.E. This area is now modern Iraq. Early civilizations, from the Egyptians to the Greeks and Romans, went on to invent more recognizable surgical tools. Surviving paintings, carvings, and other artifacts show medical instruments of surprising delicacy and sophistication. Carved from bone or wood or cast in iron or bronze, they would change little over the next 40 centuries.

As ancient civilizations developed their metalwork skills, their scalpels and other surgical instruments became more refined. Roman medical equipment preserved in the volcanic ash of Pompeii includes tools of great delicacy, many that would look familiar to surgeons today. There are forceps, probes, and amputation blades as

well as scalpels. Their handles are bronze and have indentations to increase the surgeon's grip. At either end is a blade made from iron. Surgeons preferred this metal because it was more durable than bronze or copper and could be sharpened more effectively.

Scalpels from these times would have been used for a variety of surgical procedures. Egyptian surgeons, for example, removed **abscesses** and **tumors.** In India, **cataracts** and gallstones were removed with great skill. Surgeons from all these civilizations also treated wounded soldiers. Surgery has always involved cutting, snipping, exploring, and sewing, and the tools that do this have changed little over the centuries.

Modern tools

Modern surgeons have another cutting instrument undreamed of by their predecessors, the **laser** beam. This can cut through skin or **organ** tissue in microseconds with a precision that even the finest scalpel-wielding surgeon would be unable to match. Lasers are especially effective for delicate eye operations.

In the future, scalpels and surgeons may part company. Robot arms may wield these cutting tools. Surgeons connected to their patients by video screens and Internet links may perform lifesaving operations on accident victims or battle casualties, from hundreds or even thousands of miles away.

The scalpel has been one of the surgeon's most effective tools for 5,000 years. Only time will tell if the laser beam will make it obsolete.

10,000 B.C.E.	3000 B.C.E.	50 C.E.	1962
First evidence of surgery.	Sumerians develop copper scalpel surgical instruments.	Romans use scalpels with bronze handles and durable iron blades.	The laser is first used in surgery.

Acupuncture Needles, 2000 B.C.E.

Almost all the techniques and ideas used in modern medicine can be scientifically explained. We know that pain, for example, is caused by stimulation of a nerve ending that sends a signal in the form of an electrical impulse to the brain. Chinese medicine, however, provides at least one major technique that western knowledge of the human body cannot explain. Indeed, there seems to be something almost magical about acupuncture's ability to stop pain and cure illness.

How does it work?

In acupuncture, needles are stuck into specific points along the body. The Chinese call them "meridian points," and there are 360 in total. The traditional Chinese explanation for acupuncture is that energy flows along lines in the body connecting these points. If that flow of energy is interrupted, illness follows. Inserting and twirling needles in meridian points causes the energy to flow again and heals the patient.

Acupuncture involves the use of special needles, first invented around 2000 B.C.E. Most were slivers of stone, but bronze, gold, and silver needles were also made in ancient China. As well as curing such ailments as **rheumatism** and heart disease, acupuncture can be used as an **anesthetic** during an operation.

This is a traditional set of acupuncture needles. In most acupuncture treatments there are nine needles, each of which has a different shape and use.

Out of fashion

When Europeans began to arrive in China in the late eighteenth and early nineteenth centuries, the Chinese were greatly impressed with their medical ideas and techniques. Acupuncture fell out of fashion, and for a while it was even banned.

However, acupuncturists practiced their art in secret and now it has made a comeback. It is widely used in China, not only as an anesthetic, but also to treat heart disease, **ulcers,** high blood pressure, **asthma,** and other ailments. Many modern doctors recognize its benefits. Acupuncture is now available in most developed countries and has even been used to treat mental illness.

Electric needles

Acupuncture has moved with the times. Needles are now made of stainless steel, which is more hygienic. Instead of twirling them to encourage energy flow, many acupuncturists send electric current through the needles, which seems to do the job just as effectively. Scientists are still puzzled about how acupuncture actually works. Some **skeptics** suggest that the needles are effective because the patient believes they will work, but acupuncturists have used their methods on animals with equally effective results. Another explanation is that the needles cause the body to release natural painkillers called enkephalins and endorphins into the bloodstream. These block the pathways of pain signals on the way to the brain. Although this is yet to be proven, it seems to be the most likely explanation for how this extraordinary technique works.

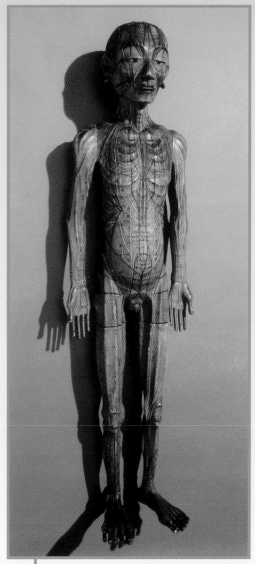

This extraordinary seventeenth-century wooden figure was made as a teaching aid for student acupuncturists. The lines along the figure show the direction and flow of energy in the body. Along the lines are 360 "meridian points" where acupuncture needles can be inserted.

2000 B.C.E.	**1822**	**1949**	**1970s to present**
First use of acupuncture.	Acupuncture is officially banned as western medicine becomes popular in China.	Communists take over China. Acupuncture is officially encouraged.	Acupuncture spreads to the west and is gradually accepted by medical authorities.

False Teeth, 700 B.C.E.

Because eating is such an essential part of human life and tooth decay and loss has been a problem from the earliest times, it is surprising that it took so long for anyone to come up with the idea of false teeth.

The first false teeth we know of were invented by the Etruscans, a culture that flourished in southern Italy before being conquered by the Romans. False teeth with gold bridgework, or clamps, to attach them to healthy teeth have been found in Etruscan tombs. They date from around 700 B.C.E. The teeth were carved from ivory or bone, or were made from second-hand human teeth.

Amazingly, there were no real advances in dentistry for the next 2,500 years. Human teeth were always in plentiful supply, especially after a war. Ivory teeth, too, continued to be used, but these rotted and turned green as regularly as real teeth did. They also tasted horrible and were expensive to replace.

Made to last

In 1770, a French chemist named Alexis Duchâteau invented porcelain false teeth, which immediately became popular. They were realistic and easy to clean and did not rot or leave a horrible taste in the mouth. On top of all that, porcelain was inexpensive. A hundred years later, advances in rubber production allowed porcelain teeth to

These gold and ivory Etruscan dentures date from around 700 B.C.E.

be mounted on a rubber plate that could be molded to fit the shape of the patient's mouth. Over the last century, false teeth have increasingly been made from plastics such as acrylic resin. This has made them even less expensive, stronger, lighter, and easier to clean.

Although false teeth allow wearers to speak and eat as though they have real teeth, they are still an uncomfortable inconvenience. Today, those who can afford it can have a full set of false teeth implants. In a procedure unimaginable before the invention of **anesthetics,** screws are drilled into the jawbone and the new teeth are set into the gum.

The dentist's drill

Around the first century C.E., doctors realized that rotting teeth did not always have to be removed. If there was only minor decay, it could be treated by drilling it out. This was not easy, however, because teeth are made of enamel, the hardest substance in the body.

The first known drill was used by a Roman surgeon named Archigenes around 100 C.E. It was powered by a rope and must have been very painful for the patient. Later drills were powered by a flywheel turned by a foot pedal, and even clockwork drills were tried.

Speed is an essential part of reducing the discomfort of drilling. Today, drills are powered by air **turbines** and revolve at an extraordinary 200,000 revolutions per minute. They are also water-cooled to reduce the heat generated by such high-speed contact with a tooth.

700 B.C.E.	1770	1851	1935
First known false teeth are made.	Porcelain false teeth are invented.	Rubber plates make false teeth comfortable to wear.	Plastic false teeth are introduced.

Artificial Limbs, 1536 C.E.

Wounds from wild animals or warfare are often fatal, but sometimes a hunter or a soldier may suffer an injury as terrible as the loss of a limb and still survive. There is evidence that this happened to the earliest human cave dwellers. The fact that the wound had time to heal shows that these people were willing to look after their injured fellow humans, even though their use to the tribe would be severely limited.

Humankind's use of tools set them apart from other creatures, even two million years ago. It was a natural step to begin using strap-on sticks and hooks as replacement legs or arms. The Greek historian Herodotus wrote about a man with a wooden foot in 500 B.C.E. Roman **mosaics** feature men with peg legs, but it was not until the sixteenth century that the first real artificial limbs were made. They were invented by an extraordinary French army surgeon named Ambroise Paré. Making use of the intricate metalwork techniques mastered by makers of armor, he began, in 1536, to make legs and arms from iron and leather. Some even had **gears** and **levers** to simulate the movement of fingers.

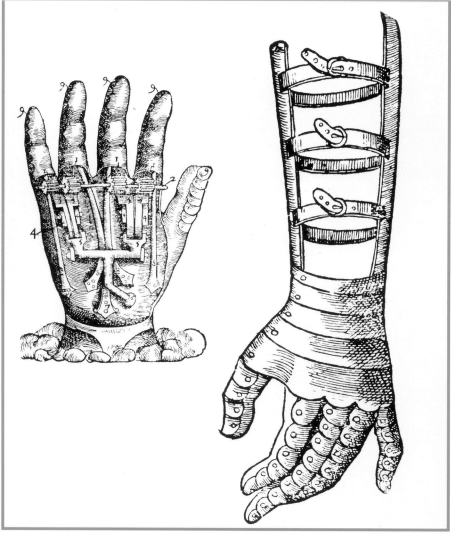

This cut-away engraving shows the gears and levers that worked the fingers in one of Paré's more ingenious artificial hands. It is taken from Paré's book of his works, Oeuvres, which was published in 1575.

Prosthetics

Paré's work laid the foundations for prosthetics, a branch of medicine concerned with artificial limbs and other **organs** such as eyeballs. Today, the most advanced artificial limbs are ingenious, complex devices. Known as myoelectric limbs, they work in the same way as human limbs, reacting to nerve impulses from the brain that tell them to move. Today, people who have lost arms or legs can dance, run, and even ski, in a way that would have made Paré and his patients gasp in astonishment.

Ambroise Paré (1517–90)

Paré learned his trade as a barber-surgeon, the lowest rank of the medical profession in sixteenth-century Europe. Such men would cut hair and shave customers, as well as perform major operations, seal wounds with boiling oil, and lance **abscesses**. This work was too dirty and unpleasant for the higher-class doctors. Although he was highly intelligent, Paré entered medicine in this way because he had a poor education and was not able to learn the Latin and Greek necessary to study medicine at a university.

As well as inventing artificial limbs, Paré also pioneered the technique of treating wounds with ointments. He invented ingenious surgical instruments and rose to become the surgeon to four kings of France. Once, when being praised for saving a patient he said, "I treated him and God healed him," words that would later be engraved on his tombstone.

*In this example of surgery in Paré's time, a soldier is having his leg amputated by an army surgeon. There was no **anesthetic** and he has been blindfolded so he can't see the procedure.*

500 B.C.E.	1536	1575	1990s
The Greek historian Herodotus records the first reference to an artificial limb.	In France, Ambrose Paré begins to make artificial limbs.	Paré's book *Oeuvres*, detailing his experience as a surgeon, is published.	Myoelectric limbs, reacting to nerve impulses are developed.

Microscope, 1590

Today, we all know that some illnesses are caused by germs, tiny **bacteria** and **viruses** that attack our body and make us feel awful. Until the microscope was invented, the tiny world of bacteria and viruses was one that could not even be imagined, let alone studied.

The most important part of a microscope is a **lens,** a piece of curved glass that magnifies whatever is seen through it. People in the earliest civilizations must have observed how a drop of water or bead of glass could make things look bigger. By the thirteenth century, glass makers had applied this knowledge to make glass lenses that could be used as eyeglasses to correct poor eyesight. Lenses always inspired superstitious mistrust among the people of medieval Europe. Anything that could not be easily understood was often dismissed as magic or witchcraft. It was not until the late sixteenth century that it occurred to anybody to use a lens to study small things.

Blurred images

Like the telescope, which uses the same basic principle, the microscope seemed to be invented in several places at once. Most historians agree that it was Zacharias Jansen who made the first microscope, in 1590. Jansen was a eyeglass-maker from Middelburg, Holland. His device magnified objects about nine times and showed a somewhat blurred image. Jansen made little use of his invention. After all, as many people reasoned at the time, what was the point in looking at small things? Fortunately for science, there were more inquisitive minds around. They took up Jansen's invention, improved it, and went on to make some of the most significant discoveries in human history.

Leeuwenhoek's microscope

In the century after Jansen's original invention, a Dutchman named Antoni van Leeuwenhoek was making his own **primitive** microscopes.

This seventeenth century microscope was owned by English scientist Robert Hooke. In Hooke's time, men would keep a microscope among the gold-trimmed books in their library. This microscope's fine leather and wood appearance was designed to fit in with the setting.

A linen merchant by trade, he had originally developed his microscope to study the quality of the cloth he bought. His device used only a single lens, but it could magnify up to 200 times. Leeuwenhoek was not an educated man, but he was endlessly curious. He used his device to unearth a world previously undreamed of.

"Animalcules"

Leeuwenhoek discovered sperm and studied the structure of muscles, eyes, arteries, and veins. He made his most important discovery when examining a speck of plaque that he had scraped from his teeth. It seemed to be made up of thousands of tiny wriggling creatures, which he called "animalcules." What Leeuwenhoek had seen were bacteria.

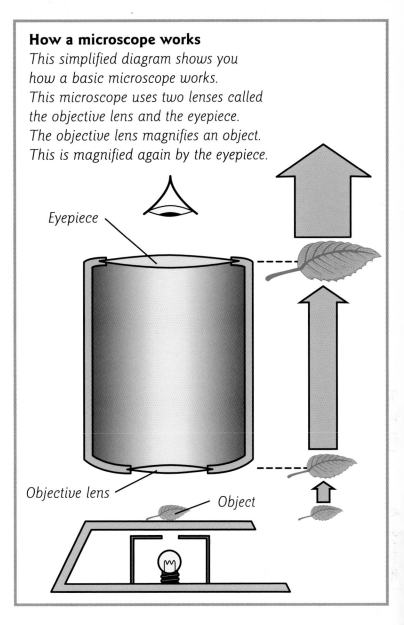

How a microscope works
This simplified diagram shows you how a basic microscope works. This microscope uses two lenses called the objective lens and the eyepiece. The objective lens magnifies an object. This is magnified again by the eyepiece.

Eyepiece

Objective lens

Object

Other, more trained scientific minds would go on to make the connection between "animalcules" and illness. Nevertheless, Leeuwenhoek had used his microscope to take humankind's first real steps in our understanding of what causes illness. Over the next four centuries, the microscope would prove to be the most invaluable tool in the fight against disease.

Thirteenth century	1590	1665	1668	1830	1861
The first eyeglasses are made from glass lenses.	Zacharias Jansen makes the first microscope.	Robert Hooke's book, *Micrographia*, has "descriptions of minute bodies made by magnifying glasses."	Antoni van Leeuwenhoek records his first use of a microscope.	Joseph Lister makes a microscope with improved lenses that magnify 2,000 times.	In France, Louis Pasteur uses a microscope to prove that bacteria cause illness.

Blood Transfusion, 1667

Loss of blood is one of the major causes of death following an accident or surgery. Replacing it with blood from other humans seems like an obvious idea, but it was not until the early seventeenth century that this was first attempted.

As with many inventions in history, there is confusion about who first performed a blood transfusion. English physician Richard Lower performed successful dog-to-dog transfusions in 1665, but some medical documents mention transfusions as early as 1630. Most people agree, though, that Jean-Baptiste Denis was the first man to perform a transfusion on a human being. Curiously, rather than taking blood from another person, he used a lamb. This was because he had had success with previous animal-to-animal transfusions.

In this seventeenth century engraving a man is transferring blood from a cow to his own body. Such animal-to-human transfusions often caused nausea and diarrhea and were sometimes fatal.

Short-lived success

Denis was a professor of philosophy and mathematics at the University of Montpellier, France. In 1667, when he was presented with a 15-year-old boy who was suffering from **lethargy** and fever, he thought a transfusion of fresh blood might cure him. Amazingly, the transfusion was a success. Although he felt a great sensation of heat in his arm during the process, Denis's patient made a remarkable recovery, regaining his previous energy and appetite for life.

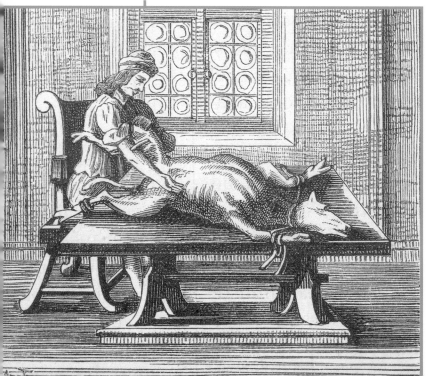

Denis's success, however, was an unexplainable exception. Most people later given animal blood suffered terrible effects. If they were lucky, they were sick. If they were unlucky, they died. These frightening failures convinced Denis he was on the wrong track. They also led to laws being passed forbidding animal-to-human transfusions and, for the moment, experimentation stopped.

Denis's failures seemed to indicate that human-to-human blood transfusion might be more successful, although this, too, was an extremely dangerous process. Throughout the nineteenth century, physicians were constantly puzzled by the hit-and-miss nature of blood transfusions. For no apparent reason, some patients died and some recovered.

Blood grouping

An Austrian physician Karl Landsteiner provided the answer. In 1901, he discovered that all human blood was not the same. He suggested there were three basic types—A, B, and O. We now know there is a fourth main type, AB. Landsteiner realized that only some blood types were **compatible.** Those that were not acted against each other, causing the body to reject the new blood it had been given.

Once this hurdle had been overcome, the future was clear for widespread use of blood transfusions. During World War II, they became commonplace and saved countless lives.

Today, blood can be given directly to patients by way of plastic blood bags, which are less likely to shatter or break than the glass bottles that were used in the past. Most countries have a system of collecting blood through volunteer donors, and new chemicals and technologies are used to keep the blood fresh and ready for use.

Recipe for blood
Blood is made up of several ingredients. Red blood **cells** carry oxygen around the body, white blood cells and platelets fight infections, and all of these float around in a liquid called plasma.

1630s	1665	1667	1818	1901	1932
Blood transfusions are first mentioned in medical records.	In England, the first dog-to-dog transfusion is successful.	The first successful animal-to-human transfusion is performed by Jean-Baptiste Denis in France.	The first successful human-to-human transfusion is performed by James Blundell.	Austrian Karl Landsteiner discovers "blood group" types.	The first blood bank is set up in Leningrad, Russia.

Stethoscope, 1819

The stethoscope is such a simple and useful tool that it is surprising that it took so long to invent! It allows a doctor to listen clearly to the movement of blood in the heart, air in the lungs, and gases in the stomach and intestines. Despite its simple design, it has proved to be one of the most useful medical inventions of all time and is still a vital tool for the modern doctor.

A French doctor named René-Théophile-Hyacinthe Laënnec was the first physician to realize that a tube would make it easier to listen to body fluids. He was a specialist in heart and lung diseases, and the noises such diseases produce are vital clues to their presence in the body.

A paper tube

One story says that Laënnec saw two boys playing with a wooden pole in the courtyard of the Louvre Palace in Paris. As one boy placed his ear to one end of the pole, the other boy scratched at the opposite end with a nail. Some time later, in 1819, Laënnec was examining a woman patient whom he suspected had a heart problem. He needed to listen to her heart, but in those days it was felt to be improper for a doctor to place his head on a woman's chest. Laënnec remembered the two boys and their pole. He rolled a piece of paper into a tube and placed this against her heart. He was delighted to realize that he could hear so clearly. He soon discovered he could hear even better with a hollow wooden tube.

Laënnec's wooden cylinder stethoscope was barely more complex than a rolled-up piece of paper, but it proved to be one of the most essential medical tools ever invented.

Improved designs

Laënnec improved the design, and the first widely used stethoscope was around 10 inches (23 centimeters) long and unscrewed in half so it could be carried in a pocket. It had a bell-like chamber at the "patient end" that helped to pick up the body's internal noises. Distinct gasps and gurgles, for example, told a doctor whether their patient had such serious ailments as **bronchitis, pneumonia,** or **tuberculosis.** In a cruel twist of fate Laënnec died of tuberculosis at age 45. The stethoscope we know today was designed in 1855 by an American doctor named George Philip Cammann. He took Laënnec's basic idea and improved it. Inside the bell-shaped chamber he added a **diaphragm** that picked up more sounds. The chamber was connected to two earpieces by a y-shaped rubber tube. The next time you visit a doctor, you will see that this design has stayed essentially the same for 150 years.

Better diagnosis

Diagnosis means the identification of a disease by looking at its signs and symptoms. In Laënnec's time, diagnosis was difficult. It was thought improper for doctors to touch their patients, aside from taking their pulse and maybe tapping their back to listen for fluid on the lungs. Instead, the patient would tell the doctor their medical history, and the doctor would make his diagnosis by what he could see, hear, and smell.

Laënnec and other physicians in Paris, one of the great medical centers of early nineteenth-century Europe, realized that a more "hands-on" approach to medicine was needed. The stethoscope helped without the doctor having to make direct physical contact. However, it took an entire century for the stethoscope to be accepted by both patients and their doctors. Queen Victoria, for example, refused to allow a doctor to use one on her.

1819	1822	1855
Laënnec records the first use of the stethoscope.	Laënnec is appointed as professor at the Collège de France.	Using Laënnec's idea, George Philip Cammann designs the modern stethoscope.

Anesthetic Inhaler, 1845

Today, we think of pain as something that can be avoided. Most painful illnesses and injuries can be soothed by drugs. Painful medical processes and procedures can be made bearable by **anesthetics,** chemicals that deaden pain. The word "anesthetic" comes from a Greek word meaning "loss of feeling."

Anesthetics have only been with us since the mid-nineteenth century. Before then, patients unlucky enough to undergo surgery were strapped to an operating table and held down by strong men. Their screams and struggling cannot have helped the surgeon, who would be judged as much for the speed of his work as for his skill.

Since the earliest times, doctors all over the world tried to discover methods to relieve the pain of surgery. In China, acupuncture was so effective that it is still used today. Elsewhere, **narcotic** drugs, hypnosis, and large amounts of alcohol all had some limited use.

This is what nineteenth-century anesthetic equipment looked like. The glass jar contains sponges soaked in ether and a tube connected to a rubber mask to allow a patient to inhale the necessary dose.

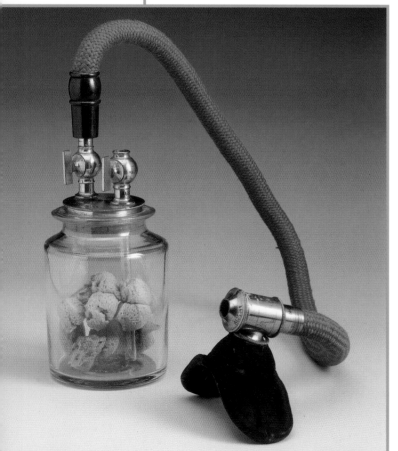

Nitrous oxide and ether

Great advances in chemistry in the late eighteenth and early nineteenth centuries provided medicine with the first effective anesthetics. The gas nitrous oxide was discovered in 1772 by Joseph Priestley in Britain. In 1799, Thomas Beddoes and Humphry Davy recognized its anaesthetizing effects, but no one thought to make use of it to deaden the pain of surgery. In 1845, American chemist Charles Jackson discovered that ether was also an effective anesthetic. It caused loss of both consciousness and feeling.

The first person to use anesthetic gas for medical purposes was an American doctor named William Morton. He used ether on a patient when he pulled a tooth in 1845. The device used to deliver the gas to the patient was a surprisingly simple invention. A sealed glass jar with an air valve contained several sponges that had been soaked in liquid ether. Connected to the jar was a long rubber tube, at the end of which was a rubber mouthpiece.

Chloroform

Ether had drawbacks, though. It had a strong, unpleasant smell and irritated the lungs. A Scottish doctor named James Young Simpson pioneered the use of another newly discovered gas, chloroform, in 1847. It was found to be a particularly useful anesthetic during childbirth. This met with strong opposition from religious extremists, who believed it was a woman's fate to suffer pain in childbirth. Opposition melted away, however, when Queen Victoria allowed the use of chloroform during the birth of her seventh child, Leopold.

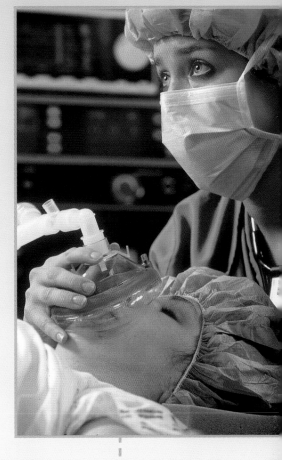

The anaesthetist is a highly skilled specialist. She sits next to the patient and monitors their condition via a computer display.

Today, the use of anesthetics in surgery is a complex medical speciality, although the way anesthetics cause loss of feeling and consciousness is still not properly understood. Highly trained doctors have a wide variety of gases and drugs to choose from, and they monitor their patients closely throughout an operation. A patient who is to undergo a major operation may have nitrous oxide gas to induce a loss of sensation, and barbiturate and neuroblocker drugs to induce sleep and muscle relaxation.

1799	1845	1846	1847	1853
Thomas Beddoes and Humphry Davy discover that nitrous oxide gas can be anesthetizing.	Ether gas is used by William Morton during a tooth extraction.	Ether gas is used by William Morton during an operation to extract a **tumor.**	Chloroform gas is used as an anesthetic by James Young Simpson.	Queen Victoria accepts chloroform during childbirth and popularizes its use.

Syringe, 1853

Like the scalpel, the syringe is an invention that is instantly associated with medicine. Giving **vaccinations,** taking blood samples, administering **anesthetics** or painkillers—all of these medical procedures are done with a syringe.

Syringes are simple pumps. They have an airtight plunger that moves up and down inside a chamber. At one end is a handle to move the plunger and at the other is a hollow needle attached to a small, rigid tube. When the plunger is drawn back, this creates a **vacuum** inside the chamber, which can suck liquid into the syringe. When the plunger is pushed down, liquid is forced out through the needle.

Who invented it?

In the nineteenth century, syringes were made of silver and glass. Today syringes are made of plastic and used only once.

The invention of the syringe had its origins in the seventeenth century. In 1657, two British scientists, Christopher Wren and Robert Boyle, invented syringe-type devices in their experiments with vacuums. Also around this time, a French army surgeon named Dominique Anel invented a syringe-like device that used suction to clean the wounds of injured soldiers. The first syringe to resemble the type we use today was invented by a French physician named Charles Pravaz in 1853. His syringe was made of silver and could hold one cubic centimeter, a very small amount, of liquid. Later in the century, glass became the preferred material for making syringes. It was easier to clean and a doctor could see at a glance how much liquid was inside it.

Today, syringes are made of clear plastic and are usually used just once and then thrown away. This is because diseases such as acquired immunodeficiency syndrome (AIDS) can be passed on through contact with an infected person's blood.

Other methods

These days, there are other ways of injecting vaccines and medicines directly into the body. The "microneedle," a small patch containing 400 tiny needles, is so small that it pierces the skin without reaching the nerve endings that register pain. The "hypospray" uses pressurized helium gas to spray powdered medicine onto the skin in a form that makes it easy to absorb. The syringe and its hollow needle remain the most common way of injecting vaccines and medicines, and taking blood and other medical fluid samples.

Protecting against disease

One of the most important uses for the syringe is for vaccinations. This is a medical procedure where a person is deliberately infected with a weak form of a **virus** (called a vaccine). This then gives them **immunity** to the more deadly version of the virus. Invented in 1796 by the English doctor Edward Jenner, vaccinations (also known as immunization or inoculation) have gone on to save millions of lives. They have wiped out or considerably diminished such diseases as smallpox, diphtheria, polio, and tetanus.

1657	1660	1853	1974
In England, Christopher Wren and Robert Boyle invent syringe-type vacuum pumps.	French surgeon Dominique Anel uses a form of syringe to clean wounds.	French doctor Charles Pravaz invents the medical syringe.	In the United States, physician Phil Brooks invents the disposable plastic syringe.

Antiseptic Spray, 1865

A patient facing an operation in the early nineteenth century had two horrors to endure—the prospect of painful surgery without **anesthetic** and the very real possibility that the operation would kill them. Those who had limbs amputated had a 50 percent chance of surviving. The high death rate following surgery was one of medicine's major mysteries.

The reason for it was simple. In those days, doctors did not know about **bacteria** and did not realize wounds could become infected. No precautions were taken to make everything clean when operating on a patient. When wounds did become infected, doctors thought the raw flesh and oozing pus were a natural part of the healing process.

A Hungarian doctor named Ignaz Semmelweis was the first person to offer a solution. He realized that infections could be carried by doctors and nurses from one patient to another. He insisted that medical staff regularly clean their hands with disinfectant. Although this procedure was very effective, it was not immediately accepted by his fellow doctors.

Carbolic acid

Someone who did pick up on Semmelweis's ideas, though, was a British surgeon named Joseph Lister. He had also studied the work of French scientist Louis Pasteur, who had recently proved that invisible bacteria were the cause of infection. Lister had noted how effectively carbolic acid, a chemical cleaner, had reduced infections among cattle. This was the germ-killer he decided to use himself.

Lister insisted on a rigorous antiseptic routine on his wards and during his operations. Instruments, dressings, and wounds were all thoroughly cleaned. Most important of all was an antiseptic spray he invented, which was directed over the patient and operating table. Looking like an intricate piece of laboratory equipment, it consisted of a water heater and a carbolic acid container. Water was heated to the boiling point, and the steam this produced was mixed with the carbolic acid. The result was a highly effective antiseptic mist that immediately led to a 300 percent drop in deadly post-operative infections.

Spreading the word

Lister published articles about his antiseptic techniques in the widely read British medical magazine, *The Lancet*. Slowly but surely, his ideas were adopted throughout the world. Lister's spray, and his equally important cleansing of instruments and dressings, made surgery much safer. By the time he died, the number of operations being performed in British hospitals had gone up by 1,000 percent.

Prevention is better

Antiseptics have drawbacks. They may kill bacteria, but they also irritate skin. Carbolic sprays were messy and unpleasant to work with. So, toward the end of the nineteenth century, surgeons began to think that preventing bacteria from getting into the wound in the first place was the way forward. All equipment and the operating room should be as sterile as possible. Rather than just cleaned, instruments were boiled to kill any bacteria on them. This is the way surgeons work today. They even wear masks to prevent bacteria from their breath reaching their patients.

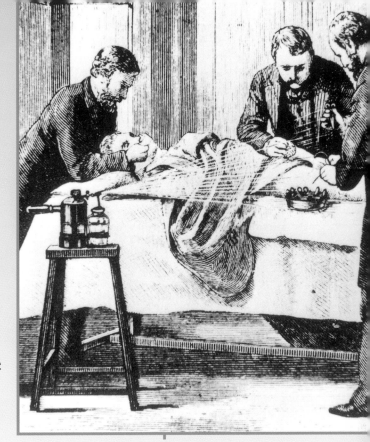

This carbolic acid spray was messy and unpleasant to work under, but it saved countless lives by preventing infection during operations.

1847	1865	1886	1900
Ignaz Semmelweis introduced antiseptic procedures to his maternity ward in Vienna.	British surgeon Joseph Lister uses carbolic acid spray during his operations.	Steam sterilization of dressings is introduced.	Use of sterile rubber gloves during surgery is introduced.

Braces, 1880

Teeth seem to be a never-ending source of discomfort for humans. Aside from the extreme pain of an **abscess,** cavity, or toothache, and the dread of the dentist's drill, there are many problems with the way teeth grow. Too many teeth or teeth growing out of position in the jaw is called malocclusion. This condition can cause anything from a lopsided smile to a swollen, deformed face.

These fixed braces use metal brackets cemented to each tooth with a wire threaded through each bracket. They are difficult to remove and can be uncomfortable at first.

Adults are supposed to have 32 teeth, spaced regularly throughout the top and bottom jaw. They should all be aligned in such a way that they fit together neatly when the jaw closes. Many of us are lucky enough to have such a set of teeth, but for those who don't, American dentist Norman W. Kingsley invented a branch of dentistry called orthodontics. The word orthodontics comes from the Greek *orthos,* meaning straight, and Latin *dens,* meaning tooth.

Kingsley was multitalented. As well as being a dentist, he was a writer, artist, and sculptor. His book *Treatise on Oral Deformities*, published in 1880, led to him being described as "the father of orthodontics."

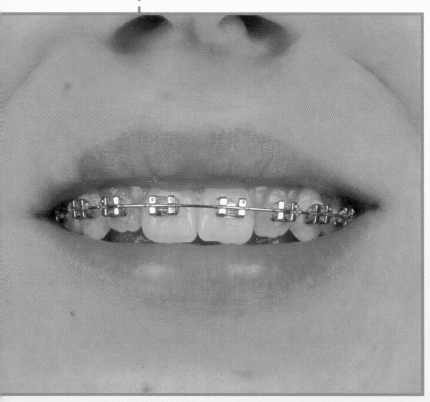

Other American dentists at the time also made major contributions to this new branch of dentistry. As well as writing a highly influential book, *A Treatise on the Irregularities of the Teeth...,* J. N. Farrar designed the first recognizably modern braces. These applied a constant, mild pressure to teeth, to gently change their position in the jaw. Finally, Edward H. Angle went on to found the first school of orthodontics at the turn of the twentieth century.

Space-age braces

The first braces were ugly, unpleasant-looking devices. They had heavy metal plates that were anchored to teeth with dental cement, and clumsy thick wires connecting them together. Some braces even had wiring that protruded from the mouth and must have made the wearer feel very self-conscious. These days, braces are made of high-tech plastics and metals, some of which were developed by NASA. The wires that slowly pull the teeth into position are stronger and more flexible and are activated by body heat. Braces today are more comfortable to wear. They also work more effectively, which cuts down on the time the patient has to wear them. For the fashion-conscious, some braces are even available in bold, bright colors!

American dentists were the pioneers in this branch of dentistry, so it seems fitting that braces are most common in the United States. Today, over four million American children and some adults wear braces in any given year.

Today, space-age technology allows light, strong, and comfortable braces that work more quickly and efficiently. They are made of material that blends with the color of the teeth and are much easier to remove than earlier braces.

1880	1901	1907
Norman W. Kingsley publishes his *Treatise on Oral Deformities*.	The American Society of Orthodontia is founded.	The first orthodontic journal is published.

Contact Lenses, 1887

Scientists have long known that light is altered when it passes through water in a glass or through a glass **lens,** and that this can be used to aid people with poor eyesight. As early as the fifth century, reading stones—glass spheres placed in front of objects—were used to help people see better. Glasses were invented in the late thirteenth century and have since become invaluable to people with poor eyesight. However, even the best ones have disadvantages. Peripheral (side) vision is poor and they can get steamed up or wet and blurred. They are inconvenient if you want to play sports, and some people feel less attractive when they are wearing them.

Early contact lenses may have freed people from the inconvenience of wearing glasses, but they were difficult to get used to and hard on the eyes.

Leonardo and Descartes

Contact lenses, which sit directly on the eye, came more than 600 years after glasses were invented. Leonardo da Vinci, an artist and inventor, is often credited with coming up with the idea. He was said to have stuck his head in a glass bowl of water and noticed how this improved his eyesight. He knew that the bowl and water were acting like a lens. In 1508, inspired by this experiment, he made sketches of small, water-filled lenses that were meant to sit directly on the eye. The French philosopher and scientist René Descartes made similar sketches. Neither man made a working model of their idea.

From glass to plastic

The first practical contact lenses were made in 1887 by a German optician named Adolf E. Fick. These were developed to correct astigmatism (distorted vision) rather than to enable the wearer to stop wearing glasses. Made of ground glass, they were so uncomfortable they could be worn only for a short time.

In 1938, a German company called Obrig and Muller made a major breakthrough when they developed plastic lenses. These were much lighter and therefore more comfortable to wear. They were much bigger than today's contact lenses and covered most of the front of the eyeball. Another breakthrough came in 1948 when Kevin Touhy of the United States devised plastic lenses that were small enough just to sit on the cornea, the front of the eye that contains the iris and pupil. These were much more comfortable.

During the 1950s and 60s, Czech scientist Otto Wichterle devised soft plastic lenses. These were first sold in 1971 by Bausch and Lomb. They were even more comfortable than the previous plastic lenses, but they were easy to damage and much more difficult to clean.

Expensive alternative

Today, contact lenses are a popular alternative to glasses, although they are generally more expensive to buy. The inconvenience of cleaning can even be avoided with disposable lenses, which are worn once, and then thrown away. These were first sold in 1997 by the pharmaceutical company Johnson and Johnson. Disposable contact lenses are twice the cost of a good pair of glasses, which might last for several years.

1508	1887	1938	1971	1997
Leonardo da Vinci draws sketches of water-filled lenses that sit on the eye.	In Germany, Adolf E. Fick invents the first glass contact lenses.	Plastic lenses are developed by the German company Obrig and Muller.	Soft contact lenses are introduced and immediately become popular.	One-day disposable contact lenses are introduced.

X-ray Machine, 1895

Fate can play funny tricks on inventors. The man who invented the microscope failed to understand how useful it could be. The man who invented antiseptics was fired from his job for encouraging his colleagues to use them. Several decades passed before their use became common practice. Wilhelm Roentgen, however, received immediate recognition for his invention, the X-ray machine, yet he stumbled across it by accident.

Roentgen was a German physicist working at the University of Würzberg. His area of research was electricity and its effects on gas-filled and **vacuum** tubes. One day in November 1895 he was passing a high voltage through a vacuum tube when he noticed that it sent out visible rays. Experiments revealed that these rays would leave traces on a photographic plate. Even more curiously, they could pass through solid objects like a box or a hand and make an image of what lay inside. He named these X-rays, because "X" was the standard scientific term for something unknown.

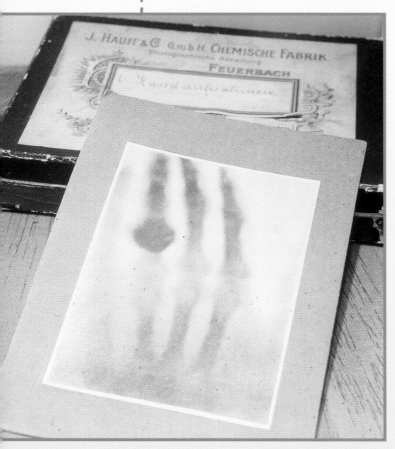

Roentgen instantly recognized these rays could be of immense use to medicine. Barely weeks after his first experiments, his invention was reported all over the world. Within three years, X-ray machines were being widely used by doctors.

Seeing inside the body

X-rays had a multitude of uses. They could show broken or diseased bones, decay in teeth, blocked arteries, fluid on the lungs and **tumors.** Making a **diagnosis** became much easier. Surgeons now knew exactly what they were looking for before they operated. X-rays had made a radical difference in the world of medicine.

Bones and foreign objects within the body showed up best of all in X-ray photographs. Soft body **organs** such as the stomach and intestine were much more difficult to see. In 1897, American physician Walter Cannon devised a "bismuth meal" that could be swallowed. It coated the stomach and intestines and showed them clearly on X-ray plates. This method is still used, although patients now swallow a chemical mix called barium sulfate, which is safer.

Healing X-rays

It was soon discovered that X-rays could also be used to treat skin diseases and **cancer.** Although they can have unpleasant side effects, they are still used to treat cancer today.

Today, X-ray film is much more sensitive than the plates used in the earliest experiments. A low-dose X-ray reveals a clear image on film in barely a second. Even so, you will notice that radiologists, doctors, and nurses who work with X-rays still leave the room whenever they make an X-ray. You are not in danger from the dose you get, but too much exposure to X-rays is harmful. If the radiologists stayed in the room they would be exposed to X-rays all day.

The most sophisticated X-ray machines used today are called CAT (Computer Axial Tomography) scanners. They take a whole series of X-rays and produce a detailed three-dimensional image for doctors to study.

How a body scanner works

A modern computer axial tomography (CAT) scanner can produce three-dimensional images of the inside of the body. A patient must lie very still on the couch for up to 30 minutes. A computer puts together all the information, which can then be studied on a video screen.

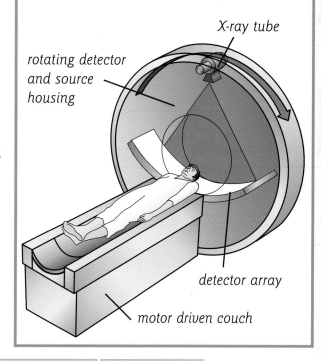

X-ray tube

rotating detector and source housing

detector array

motor driven couch

1895	1897	1901	1914	1975
In Germany, Wilhelm Roentgen discovers X-rays.	Walter Cannon devises a "bismuth meal" to make soft body tissue visible to X-rays.	Wilhelm Roentgen is awarded the Nobel Prize for physics.	X-ray machines are in common use around the world.	CAT scans, 3-D X-rays, are introduced in hospitals.

For thousands of years, the most common way of coping with hearing loss was to use some form of ear trumpet. This was a tube with a large opening at one end that caught incoming sounds and **transmitted** them to a small earpiece at the other end of the tube. You can get some idea of how they worked by cupping your hands behind your ears. You will instantly be aware that background sounds are louder, and that you can hear noises you had not previously noticed.

The first portable electric hearing aid, the Otophone, was very different from the tiny hearing aids of today. Worn inside the ear, the Otophone weighed 15 pounds (7 kilograms) and had to be carried around in a small case!

The earliest known types of ear trumpets were made of the hollowed-out horn of a cow or ram. Over the centuries people experimented with various other types of materials, such as wood, brass, silver, and shell. In the early nineteenth century, one of the most elaborate ear trumpets was made for the Portuguese king, John VI. He had a throne made with armrests in the shape of snarling lions' heads. Courtiers knelt and spoke into the lions' mouths and the sound was carried by tubes into the king's ears.

Hearing through teeth

One hearing aid, used in the late nineteenth century, was called the Dentaphone. It was shaped like a fan and held in the teeth. The wearer leaned forward to catch the sound of someone speaking to them. The vibrations of the voice were caught by the fan and transmitted through the teeth to the skull and the ear. It worked well enough to become a common hearing aid in the nineteenth century.

Hidden aids

Other hearing devices of that time tried to be more discreet. One consisted of a table with a vase of flowers. Hidden in the flowers was a large horn. A tube from the horn led through the vase and table out to the side, where the deaf person would listen to the conversation with a small earpiece. It was not a success. The listener had to be sitting down to use it, and the person speaking to them had to shout into the flowers. Other aids included ear trumpets concealed in top hats and even tiaras!

Telephone and radio

In the late nineteenth century the famous inventor Alexander Graham Bell was experimenting with hearing devices for deaf children when he came up with the telephone. Another inventor, Miller Reese Hutchinson, made use of Bell's ideas and invented the first electric hearing aid in 1901. He called it the Telephone Transmitter. It had a microphone to catch sound and turn it into an electrical signal, an **amplifier** to make the signal stronger, and an earpiece which turned the signal back into sound.

These, and other similar devices, were as bulky and awkward to use as the previous non-electric ear trumpets. The real breakthrough came in 1923, when the Marconi company invented the Otophone. It was packed into a case weighing 15 pounds (7 kilograms), but it was small and light enough to be carried around.

Today, miniature hearing aids use **microchip** and **digital** technology. They are so small they can be worn inside the ear canal and adjusted by remote control.

1901	1920	1923	1935	1952
Miller Reese Hutchinson invents the first electric hearing aid.	Earl Charles Hanson's vactuphone uses valve technology.	Marconi introduces the Otophone, the first portable electric hearing aid.	A. Edwin Steven develops an electric hearing aid small enough to be worn on the body.	Sonotone produces the first transistorized hearing aid, small enough to be worn behind the ear.

Iron Lung, 1928

Imagine being trapped inside a coffin-sized iron box with only your head poking out of the end. As you lie there, leather bellows wheeze up and down, forcing air in and out. It sounds like a nightmare, but for many children in the mid-twentieth century, it was a lifesaver. The box, nicknamed the "iron lung," helped people who could no longer breathe to stay alive.

In the first half of the twentieth century, a **virus** called **polio** claimed thousands of lives. It lurked in contaminated food or water and paralyzed the nerves that controlled the limbs or lungs. If the lungs were affected, the victim could **suffocate** within hours. Children were particularly vulnerable to polio, which made it one of the most feared diseases of the time. What was needed was some sort of breathing device that could keep a child alive for a few vital days until the effects of the virus wore off and they could breathe again.

Cat in a box

In 1926, the Rockefeller Institute, a charitable organization, began research into ways of saving polio victims. One member of the team was physician Philip Drinker. His brother was researching the way animals breathe. As part of this research he constructed a sealed box in which to place a cat, to observe how much air it breathed in and out. Drinker realized a similar device could actually help people to breathe.

He designed a box that was large enough for a human and used a modified **vacuum** cleaner to pump air in and out of it. When air was pumped out, this caused a person's chest to rise, and air was drawn into the lungs. When air was pumped in, the chest fell, and air was expelled from the lungs.

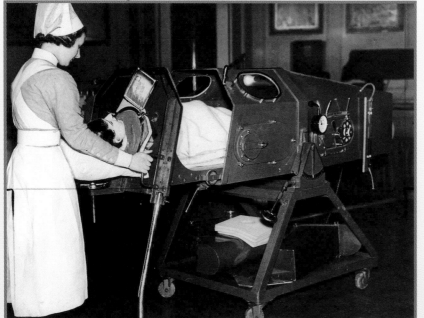

This is a young victim of polio inside an iron lung. A rubber seal around the patient's neck kept the iron box air-tight.

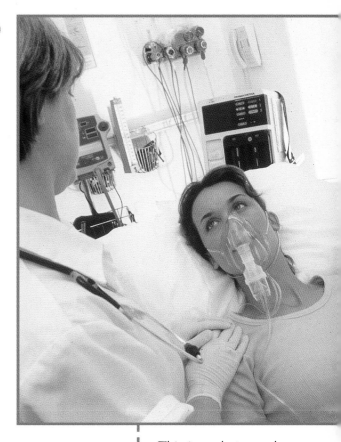

Other inventors

Drinker's iron lung was the first breathing device to be used in hospitals, but a similar idea was originally suggested by a Scottish doctor, named John Dalziel, in 1832. The inventor of the telephone, Alexander Graham Bell, designed a "vacuum jacket" respirator in 1881, after his newborn son had died with breathing difficulties. Nether idea was developed further.

Saving lives

In 1928, Drinker's device was tried out on an unconscious eight-year-old girl who could barely breathe and was near death. She regained consciousness within minutes and was soon asking for ice cream. The iron lung obviously worked, although its first patient died soon afterwards of **pneumonia.** By 1931, the iron lung was being produced commercially and became a common sight in hospitals all over the world.

Today, a face mask and a small ventilator are used to help patients suffering from serious breathing disorders. Only a few hospitals still have iron lungs. However, between the 1930s and the 1950s, these clumsy and rather scary-looking devices saved thousands of lives.

1832	1881	1928	1931	1954
John Dalziel first suggests idea of sealed box to help patients with breathing difficulties.	Alexander Graham Bell designs "vacuum jacket."	Philip Drinker invents the "iron lung."	Iron lung sold all over the world	First successful polio vaccine is introduced.

Electron Microscope, 1933

The invention of the microscope in 1590 brought huge advances in medicine over the next three centuries. It was an essential tool in the discovery of **bacteria** that caused diseases, yet, even today, the most powerful ordinary microscopes can only magnify up to 2,500 times. By the early twentieth century, scientists were wondering how they could see into the even smaller dimensions of the microscopic world.

A German scientist named Ernst Ruska came up with the answer. In 1933, he devised a magnifying device called an electron microscope. An ordinary microscope uses **lenses** and light to examine an object. Ruska's microscope used a stream of electrons, tiny particles that help make up **atoms.** These electrons bounced off the object being examined and onto a detector, which used the information to make an image on a television screen.

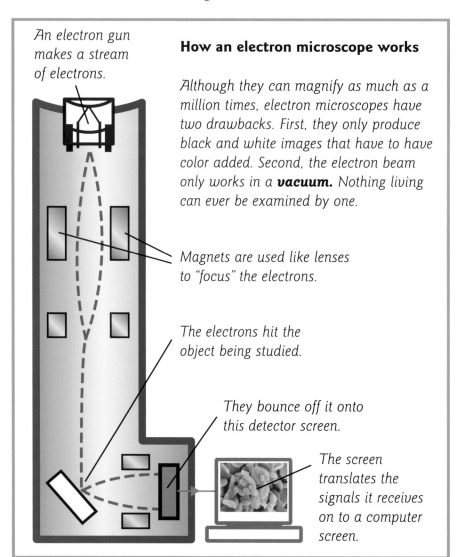

An electron gun makes a stream of electrons.

How an electron microscope works

Although they can magnify as much as a million times, electron microscopes have two drawbacks. First, they only produce black and white images that have to have color added. Second, the electron beam only works in a **vacuum.** Nothing living can ever be examined by one.

Magnets are used like lenses to "focus" the electrons.

The electrons hit the object being studied.

They bounce off it onto this detector screen.

The screen translates the signals it receives on to a computer screen.

At first, Ruska's invention could only magnify up to ten times, about the same amount as Zacharias Jansen's first microscope. It soon improved, however, and within a year, Ruska's microscope was magnifying images thousands of times greater than an ordinary microscope could achieve. In 1938, the Siemens electronic company began to sell the electron microscope commercially. Another medical breakthrough was just around the corner.

Mysterious germs

Ordinary microscopes had revealed that diseases such as **pneumonia** and **bronchitis** were caused by particular bacteria. However, the germs that caused other illnesses, such as measles and rabies, could still not be found. This is because they were caused by **viruses,** the smallest living things known to science. Some viruses are a million times smaller than bacteria. Using an electron microscope, scientists soon discovered these deadly killers. Once they knew what they were dealing with, they could devise medicines to fight the viruses.

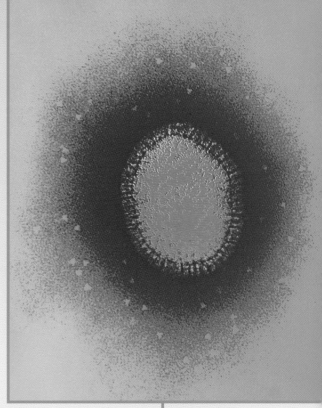

This electron microscope picture shows flu viruses. The image is magnified about 137,000 times.

Electron microscopes have proved invaluable in other areas of medical research, too. Like ordinary microscopes, they provide scientists with vital clues to the life processes of the body. An image from an electron microscope also helped scientists Francis Crick and James Watson to make one of the most important discoveries of the twentieth century—the structure of **DNA,** the material that makes up our **genes.**

Today, the electron microscope is just one of the tools used by medical research scientists. Scanning tunneling microscopes have a minute needle that records changes in electric currents between the needle and the surface being examined. In other microscopes, sound waves, X-rays, magnetic forces, or minute changes in temperature build up information which is then shown as an image on a computer screen.

1590	1933	1938	1953	1981
The light microscope is invented.	German Ernst Ruska invents the electron microscope.	The Siemens electronic company sells the electron microscope commercially.	The electron microscope helps James Watson and Francis Crick discover the structure of DNA.	The scanning tunneling microscope is perfected.

Genetic Engineering, 1973

The "double helix" of DNA looks like a spiral staircase. It contains sequences of four proteins that make up a chemical code for each of the body's genes.

The health of every person on the planet is closely connected to their **genes**—complex sets of chemical instructions in our **cells** that are made up of a substance called **DNA.** Humans have about 30,000 genes. They tell the body how to build itself and how to act. They decide how tall someone is and whether they are likely to develop a particular illness such as **cancer.**

In 1953, James Watson of the United States and Englishman Francis Crick discovered the structure of DNA. Once this structure was understood, scientists could then began inventing ways to change genes in living things. This is called **genetic engineering,** and it is likely to have a major effect on all aspects of medicine.

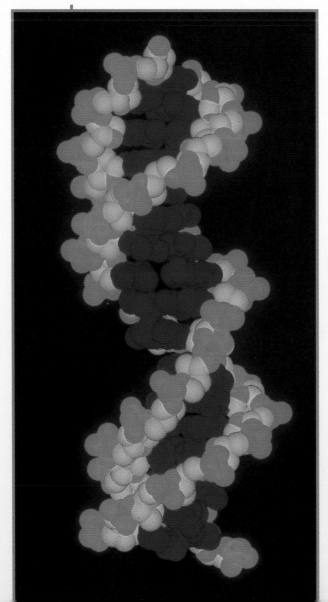

How it began

In 1973, American biochemists Stanley Cohen and Herbert Boyer took the first steps in genetic engineering when they cut a strand of **bacteria** DNA at a specific point and inserted a gene from another living thing into it.

In the world of medicine, genetic engineering allows scientists to invent new types of plants and animals that can be used to treat illness. For example, a type of bacteria has been engineered that produces insulin, which diabetics need to stay alive.

The entire sequence of every one of the human body's genes, called the genome, has also been recorded. This will have a huge impact on scientists' understanding of how to detect and cure illnesses.

Therapy

Research is currently being conducted on the introduction of specific genes into the body to cure illnesses such as cystic fibrosis. This is called gene therapy. Scientists are also investigating the possibility of curing inherited diseases, such as sickle cell anemia, by altering the genetic makeup of people who carry the genes that cause these illnesses. This is called germline therapy.

Genetic engineering is still a very young science, and many of its most recent breakthroughs are yet to have an impact on medicine. Now, the possibilities seem endless, but only time will tell whether genetic engineering lives up to its promises.

Differences in healthy and unhealthy genes show up as different colors and shades on a computer screen. These genes are unhealthy, so they are brighter than they would be if they were healthy.

Cloning

In 1996, scientists in Scotland **cloned** a sheep they named Dolly. They did this by taking a body cell from an adult sheep and using its DNA to make an exact copy of that sheep. In the future, cloning could allow scientists to produce tailor-made body **organs** for transplant patients, or create whole herds of cows or sheep that produce useful drugs in their milk. The technique could also be used to enable infertile couples to have a child who would be a clone of one of them.

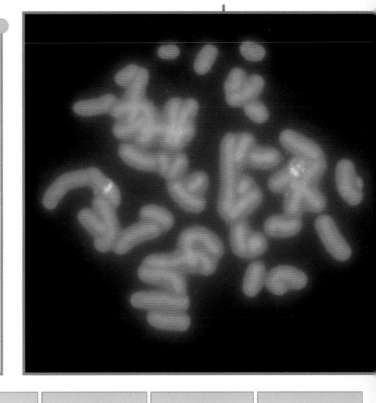

1953	1973	1986	1990	1996	2000
James Watson and Francis Crick discover the structure of DNA.	Stanley Cohen and Herbert Boyer perform the first genetic engineering with bacteria.	The human genome project is set up to list the sequence of the entire human genome.	The first trials for "gene therapy" are conducted.	Dolly, a cloned sheep, is created by the Roslin Institute in Scotland.	The first draft of the human genome is published.

MRI Scanner, 1977

Although X-ray pictures, especially three-dimensional CAT scans, are helpful, they can only see so much. Right from the start, it was clear that X-rays would always show solid parts of the body, such as bones, much better than softer parts. Medical scientists are always searching for better ways of seeing inside the body. In 1977, another major breakthrough was made when the Magnetic Resonance Imaging (MRI) scanner was invented.

Raymond Damadian of the United States led the team that built the scanner. Like an X-ray machine, it can look into the body and "see" bones, but it is especially good at showing soft tissue (such as the brain) or body tissue inside bones (such as the spinal column). It is not as good at examining the heart or lungs, because their movement blurs the image the scanner produces.

History

The origins of the MRI scanner go back to 1945, when scientists discovered that **atoms** in an object placed inside a magnetic field give off signals called radio waves. They called this phenomenon nuclear magnetic resonance (NMR). In the 1950s, an NMR researcher named Felix Bloch stuck his finger in the laboratory apparatus and discovered it gave off a strong signal. Bloch quickly realized that NMR could be used to examine the insides of people's bodies. In 1971, building on this research, Damadian used NMR apparatus to detect a **tumor** in a **cancer** patient. The idea worked so well that he went on to build a scanner capable of examining a whole body. The scanner looks like a big box with a hole in the middle for the patient to lie in. It uses powerful magnets to produce radio signals in the body. It then detects these signals and turns them into an image on a television screen.

In this MRI of a patient's head, you can clearly see the brain, the airway passage inside the nose, and the tongue.

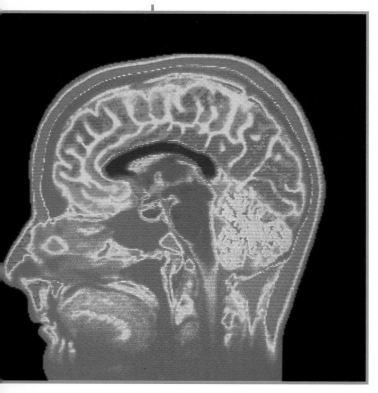

40

Harmless

Unlike X-rays, which expose the body to very small doses of harmful **radioactivity,** the MRI scanner seems to be completely harmless and pain-free. It also produces almost instant images. It does have disadvantages for a patient, though. Being placed inside a scanner, which makes loud clanking noises, can be an unpleasant experience. The scanning process can also take anything from 30 to 60 minutes, during which the patient must lie completely still. Because very strong magnets are used, patients with metal clips or devices inside their body, such as a heart pacemaker, cannot be examined.

MRI scanners are painless to the patient, although some people find being in one can be an unpleasant experience.

Other scanners

Aside from X-rays and MRI, there are other ways of looking inside the body. One method, called positron emission tomography (PET), introduces a mild radioactive substance into a patient, which is then picked up by a scanner. This is particularly useful for examining digestive **organs** such as the stomach. Another technique is called ultrasound. This makes a picture on a television screen by detecting sound waves inside a person.

1945	1971	1977	1984
Nuclear magnetic resonance is discovered.	Raymond Damadian uses NMR apparatus to detect a tumor.	The first MRI scanner is built. It can produce a whole body image.	MRI scanners are approved for use in medicine and are sold to hospitals around the world.

Endoscope and Camera, 1982

Despite huge advances in surgical techniques and safety, making an opening in a human body to perform surgery is always uncomfortable and risky. Recently, however, medical scientists have developed techniques that allow a surgeon to operate inside a patient while only making a tiny **incision.** This is called laparoscopic surgery, and it was developed thanks to an invention called the endoscope, a tube used to look inside the human body.

The first endoscope dates from 1806, when an Austrian physician named Philip Bozzini built a device he called the "Lichtleiter." A candle was used to provide illumination, but the device was never used on people. Over the next few decades the idea was developed further, but it only really came into its own with the arrival of **fiber-optic** technology.

In 1930, a German medical student named Heinrich Lamm suggested using glass fibers to examine the inside of the human body. His idea was ahead of its time. The quality of the glass used in the 1930s was too poor to give a good image. Improvements in quality after World War II led to the development of glass-fiber endoscopes in the 1960s.

This is a keyhole surgery camera in action. The surgeon can see what he needs to do on the TV monitor.

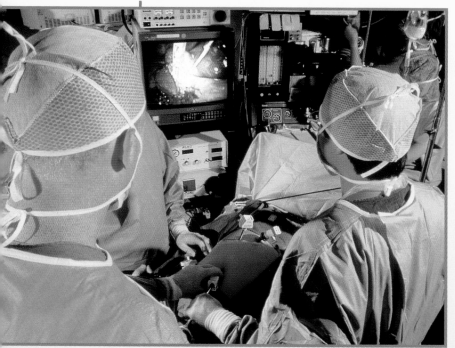

Adding a camera

In 1982, a miniature camera was fitted to an endoscope. This let surgeons see what they were doing by looking at a video monitor rather than peering into the eyepiece of the endoscope. It also allowed what they saw to be recorded on videotape. In 1996, a live operation was "broadcast" over the Internet, using this kind of camera.

Fiber optics

The idea of fiber optics, thin rods of glass that carry light, came about in the 1840s when it was noticed that light bent along the curve of water in a fountain. The idea was developed over the century and was put to practical use in 1900 with a forerunner of the modern endoscope. This was a curved quartz rod that was used in dentistry to light up the inside of the mouth. In the 1960s and 70s very pure glass fibers were developed that could carry light over long distances with very little loss or distortion. Today, millions of miles of fiber-optic cables carry Internet, telephone, and television signals all around the world. A single fiber can carry 200 television channels and 200,000 phone conversations.

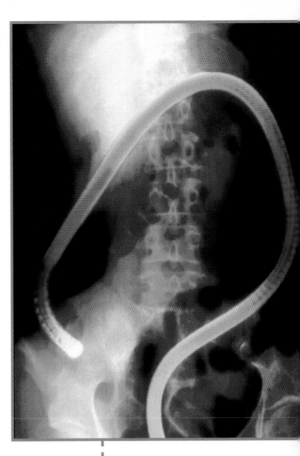

This colored X-ray shows an endoscope inside a patient's **abdomen.** *The bones of the spine can also be seen in green.*

Today, endoscopes are an important part of a surgeon's examination and operating equipment. Most endoscopes hold two fiber-optic tubes, which run from one end to the other. One tube carries light into the body, while the other has a **lens** at one end that carries the image.

Doctors use an endoscope to examine such areas as the inside of the nose and the digestive system. The endoscope also allows doctors to perform surgery by making an opening in the body only 1/2 to 3/4 inch (1–2 centimeters) wide. Some endoscopes have their own miniature surgical instruments attached. One recent use of the endoscope is to send a **laser** beam down it to burn away **tumors** or repair body tissue.

1806	1930	1960s	1982	1996
Philip Bozzini builds the first endoscope.	Heinrich Lamm suggests using glass fibers for medical examination.	Glass fiber endoscopes are first used.	A miniature camera is fitted to an endoscope.	A live operation is "broadcast" on the Internet using a camera in an endoscope.

Timeline

10,000 B.C.E.	First evidence of surgery.
3000 B.C.E.	Sumerians develop the copper scalpel.
2000 B.C.E.	First known use of acupuncture needles.
700 B.C.E.	First known false teeth.
1508 C.E.	Leonardo da Vinci draws sketches of water-filled lenses that sit on the eye.
1536	Ambroise Paré invents artificial limbs.
1590	Zacharias Jansen makes the first microscope.
1667	The first successful animal-to-human blood transfusion is performed by Jean-Baptiste Denis.
1770	Porcelain false teeth are invented.
1818	The first successful human-to-human blood transfusion is performed by James Blundell.
1819	Laënnec is the first doctor to use a stethoscope.
1845	Ether gas is used by William Morton as an **anesthetic** during a tooth extraction.
1847	Chloroform gas is used as an anesthetic by James Young Simpson.
1853	Charles Pravaz invents the medical syringe.
1861	Louis Pasteur proves that **bacteria** cause illness.
1865	Joseph Lister uses carbolic acid spray during operations.
1880	Norman W. Kingsley publishes *Treatise on Oral Deformities*.

1887	Adolf E. Fick invents glass contact lenses.
1895	Wilhelm Roentgen discovers X-rays.
1900	Sterile rubber gloves are first used during surgery.
1901	Miller Reese Hutchinson invents the electric hearing aid.
1923	The first portable electric hearing aid is introduced.
1928	Philip Drinker invents the "iron lung."
1933	Ernst Ruska invents the electron microscope.
1953	James Watson and Francis Crick discover the structure of **DNA.**
1954	The first successful **polio** vaccine is introduced.
1960s	**Fiber-optic** endoscopes are first used.
1973	Stanley Cohen and Herbert Boyer carry out the first test of **genetic engineering.**
1974	Phil Brooks invents the disposable plastic syringe.
1975	CAT scans are introduced in hospitals.
1977	The first MRI scanner is built.
1982	A miniature camera is fitted to an endoscope.
1996	A **cloned** sheep named Dolly is created at the Roslin Institute in Scotland.
1997	One-day disposable contact lenses are introduced.
2000	The first draft of the Human Genome Project is published.

Glossary

abdomen part of the body below the chest, containing the intestines

abscess area of the body filled with pus

amplifier in hearing aids, a device used to make an electrical signal stronger

anesthetic substance that causes loss of sensation in the body, especially loss of pain

asthma medical condition where a patient has difficulty breathing and feels tightness in the chest

atom minute particle that makes up the basic building blocks of matter

bacteria tiny organisms, many of which cause disease

bronchitis illness that affects the lungs and causes coughing and difficulty breathing

cancer often fatal growth in the body caused by body cells dividing uncontrollably

cataract clouding of the lens of the eye, which causes vision problems

cell tiny section that makes up the various parts of a plant or animal

clone living thing that is genetically identical to another living thing because it has been produced with the same DNA

compatible capable of existing together

diagnosis identification of a disease based on the examination of particular symptoms

diaphragm muscular partition between the chest and the abdomen

digital representing information in numerical form, most often used by computers

DNA chemical code that is found in a gene

fiber optics transmission of light down flexible, transparent tubes of glass

gear toothed wheel used in machinery to change the speed or direction of a mechanism

genes set of chemicals passed on when living things reproduce that determine the shape and character of their offspring

genetic engineering science of changing the shape and character of living things by altering their genes

immunity ability of the body to fight off particular illnesses

incision cut made with a scalpel during surgery

laser machine that produces a very intense beam of light

lens piece of transparent material, such as glass, that can bend light and can be used to make things look bigger or clearer

lethargy extreme tiredness and weakness

lever rigid bar that is part of the mechanism of a machine. Levers usually transfer a force from one part of the machine to another.

microchip tiny piece of electrical machinery used in computers

mosaic small pieces of glass, wood, or stone that are arranged to form a larger picture

narcotic something that dulls the senses and causes drowsiness

organ part of the body, such as the heart, brain, or liver, that performs a specific function

pneumonia disease in which the lungs fill with fluid

polio disease that causes paralysis, especially in the limbs and lungs

primitive something in an early stage of development

radioactivity particles or rays given off by atoms of particular materials

rheumatism medical condition with symptoms that include painful joints and muscles

skeptic someone who questions ideas, especially new ideas

suffocate to die because of a lack of oxygen

transmit to pass on, often said of an illness caused by a bacteria or virus

trepanning ancient medical practice in which holes were drilled in the skull, supposedly to release evil spirits that were causing an illness

tuberculosis disease that causes swellings in the lungs

tumor swelling in the body caused by an abnormal growth of cells

turbine wheel with blades inside a machine or engine that can be rotated at very high speed

ulcer sore on the skin or an organ that heals very slowly

vaccination deliberate introduction into the body of a bacteria or virus that causes a mild form of a disease. This gives the body immunity to the more deadly form of this disease.

vacuum space that contains nothing, not even air

virus extremely small organism that causes illnesses

More Books to Read

Casanellas, Antonio. *Great Discoveries & Inventions that Improved Human Health.* Milwaukee: Gareth Stevens Incorporated, 2000.

Jennings, Gael. *Bloody Moments: Highlights from the Astounding History of Medicine.* Toronto, Ont.: Annick Press, Limited, 2000.

Woods, Michael, and Mary B. Woods. *Ancient Medicine: From Sorcery to Surgery.* Minneapolis: The Learner Publishing Group, 1999.

Index